SPHINX

The Story of a Caterpillar
Newly Revised Edition

Robert M. McClung

Illustrated by
Carol Lerner

William Morrow and Company
New York   1981

Printed in the United States of America.
1   2   3   4   5   6   7   8   9   10

Library of Congress Cataloging in Publication Data

McClung, Robert M
   Sphinx: the story of a caterpillar.
   Summary: Details a year in the life of a sphinx moth,
which is known as the horned tomato worm in its caterpillar stage.
1. Caterpillars—Juvenile literature. [1. Caterpillars]
I. Lerner, Carol. II. Title.
QL561.S7M32   1981   595.78′1   80-27362
ISBN 0-688-00464-4   ISBN 0-688-00465-2 (lib. bdg.)

The June sun was shining down bright and clear on
the big garden. The ground was warm, and everything
was growing fast.

Peavines were climbing up the fence, and the lettuce
leaves were getting bigger and bigger. There was more
lettuce than the garden slugs could eat.

The early sweet corn had sprouted, and its pale
curled leaves glistened with dew. The gardener had put
a scarecrow between the rows to keep the birds away.
Some birds don't scare easily, though.

The beans were sprouted, and each bean had pushed its way aboveground, anchored by the root. Tiny heart-shaped leaves were unfolding above each half bean. The rabbits would have had a feast if they could have gotten through the fence.

One did.

The tomato plants were growing fast too. The gardener had set them out just a week ago. On the last tomato plant in the row, there were four tiny objects on the underside of the leaves. They hadn't been there the day before.

They looked like eggs. They were smooth and almost round. But they were tiny, like the head of a pin, and pale green in color.

Still, they *were* eggs.

What kind of eggs?

Not birds' eggs, for they were too small.

Not fish eggs, for they were not in the water.

They were insect eggs. Lots of insects lay eggs.

In the evening a beetle started to investigate one of the eggs, but a big toad snapped up the beetle before it could do anything to it.

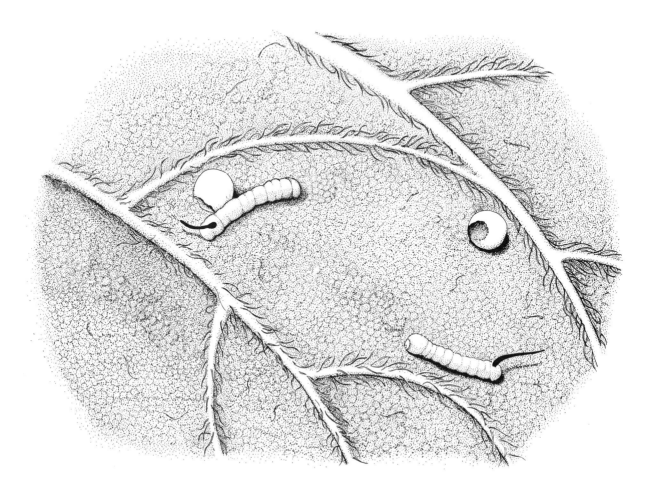

A few days later a tiny line appeared around the top of that egg. Something inside was cutting a cap in the shell so it could get out. Soon the cap pushed up, and a tiny caterpillar crawled out. Caterpillars hatched from the other three eggs too.

They were very small—no more than a quarter of an inch long. Their color was pale green. Each one had a long threadlike horn near the end of its body.

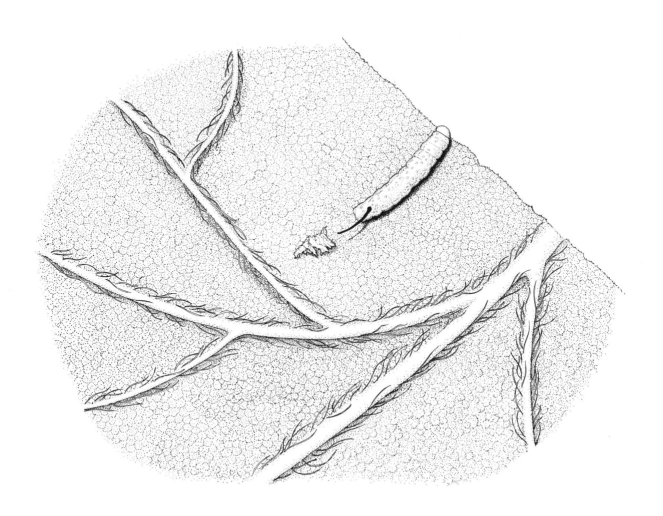

The little caterpillars began to eat tomato leaves
right away, and they grew—and grew—and grew.
After several days they had eaten so much that
their skins were tight, like suits that are too small.
Then the skin of each one split down the back,
and each caterpillar crawled out of the old skin.
There was a new, looser skin underneath—
more room to grow!

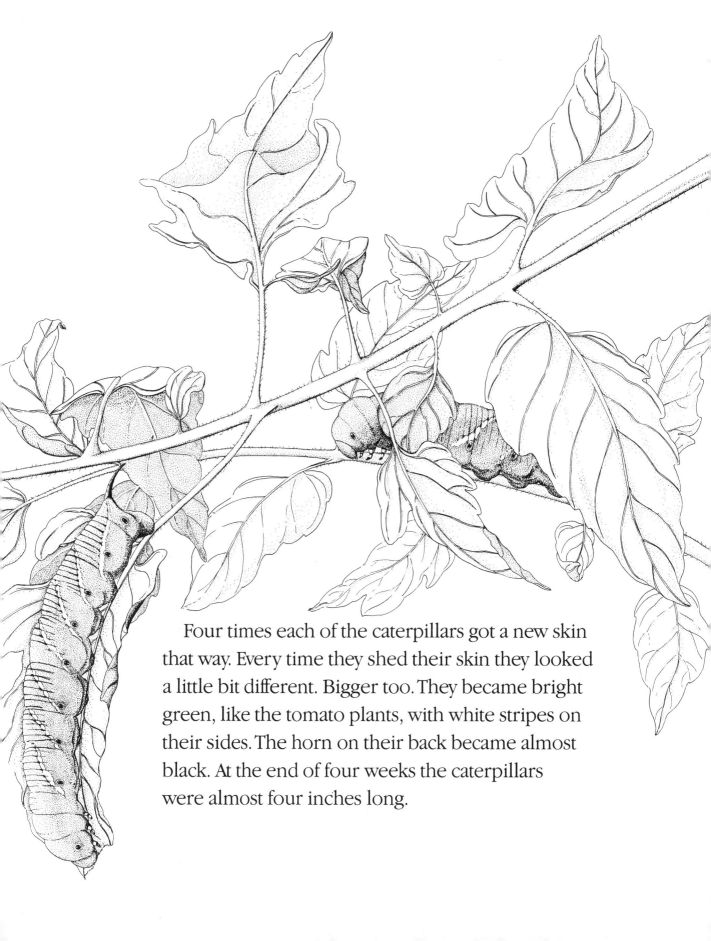

Four times each of the caterpillars got a new skin
that way. Every time they shed their skin they looked
a little bit different. Bigger too. They became bright
green, like the tomato plants, with white stripes on
their sides. The horn on their back became almost
black. At the end of four weeks the caterpillars
were almost four inches long.

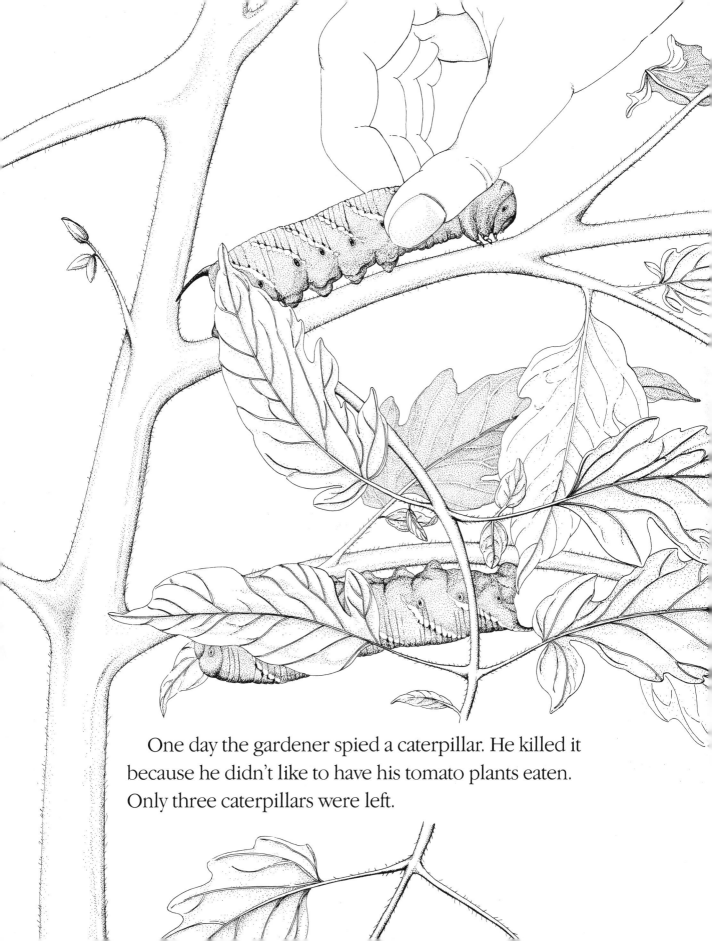

One day the gardener spied a caterpillar. He killed it
because he didn't like to have his tomato plants eaten.
Only three caterpillars were left.

The next day a big bird found another one and ate it.
Then there were only two left. Two caterpillars–eating
more tomato leaves.

A little wasp laid her eggs under the skin of one of
them. These eggs hatched into tiny wormlike grubs
inside the caterpillar. The grubs ate the inside of the
caterpillar until they were ready to spin cocoons. Then
they wriggled out and spun their little white cocoons
on the caterpillar's back. That caterpillar died. Only one
was left.

He went right on eating tomato leaves. He was plump and fat from eating so much.

If something disturbed the caterpillar, he would rear up his head threateningly and swing the front part of his body from side to side. Sometimes he made a clicking noise with his jaws.

You might think he was ferocious. But he wasn't at all. You might think he could bite or sting with his horn, but he couldn't.

When the caterpillar reared up, he looked something like the great Sphinx in Egypt. So he was called Sphinx too.

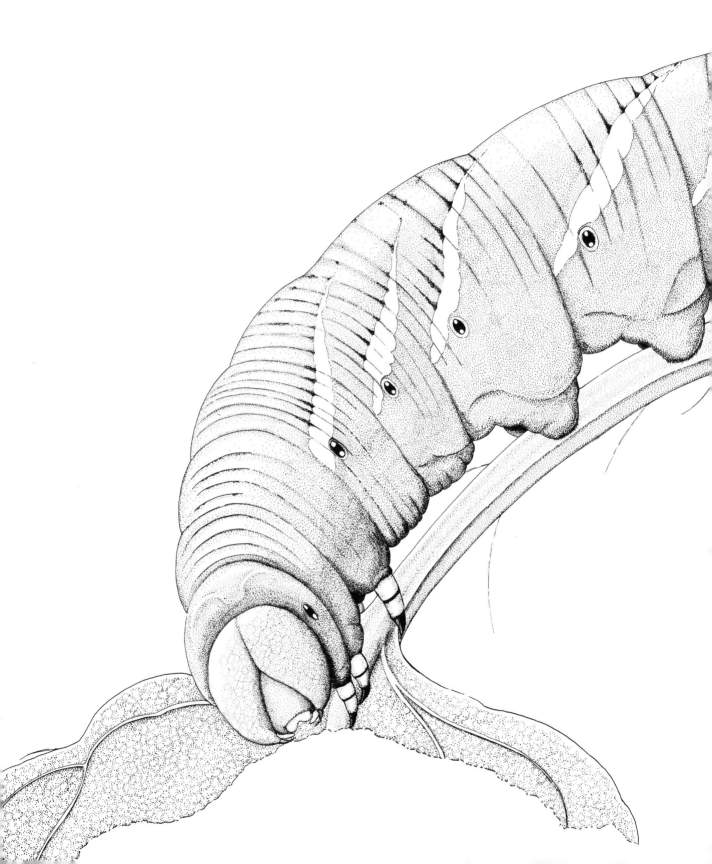

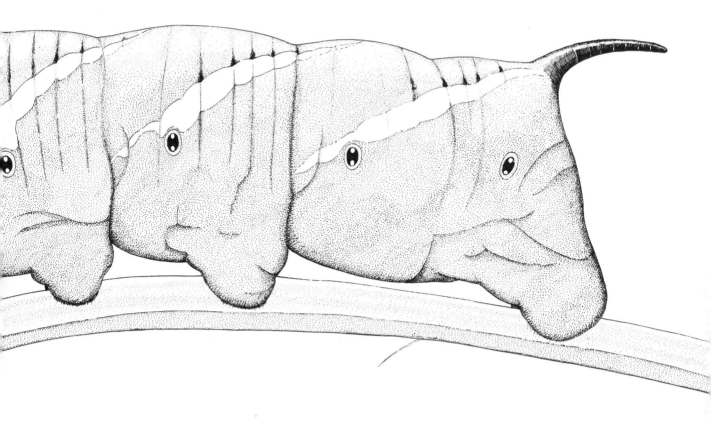

Sphinx breathed through a series of tiny holes, called
"spiracles," on his sides. When he was eating, he held
the tomato leaf with his six tiny true legs, just under his
head. He clung to the branch with five pairs of fleshy
limbs called "prolegs." They were not real legs at all, but
Sphinx caterpillar used them as legs while he had them.

Sphinx's tiny jaws opened sideways, like a pair of
scissors. He always started eating by stretching his head
up to the edge of the leaf and eating downward toward
his body. Up and down. Up and down. Finally Sphinx
had eaten enough.

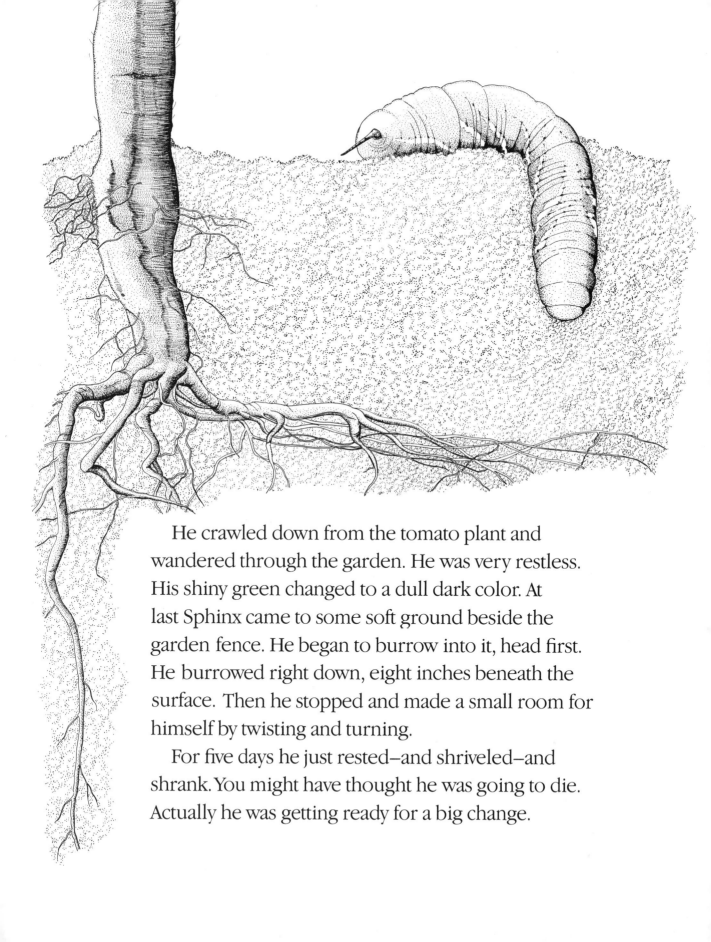

He crawled down from the tomato plant and
wandered through the garden. He was very restless.
His shiny green changed to a dull dark color. At
last Sphinx came to some soft ground beside the
garden fence. He began to burrow into it, head first.
He burrowed right down, eight inches beneath the
surface. Then he stopped and made a small room for
himself by twisting and turning.

For five days he just rested—and shriveled—and
shrank. You might have thought he was going to die.
Actually he was getting ready for a big change.

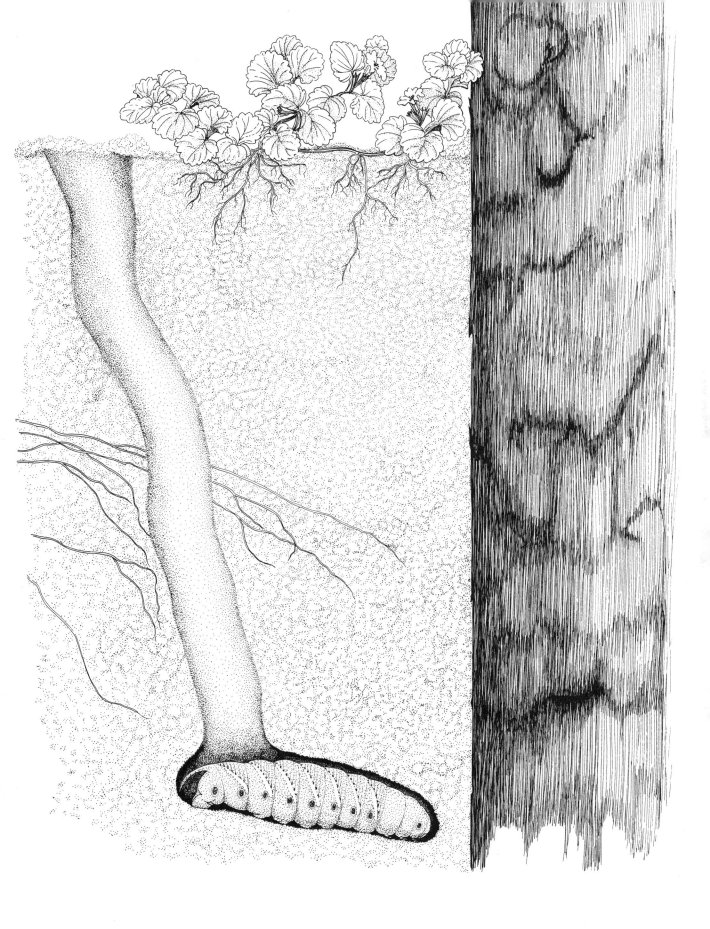

Then his skin split down the back again. But it was no caterpillar that wriggled out of the old skin this time. Sphinx had changed into a smooth pupal case–with a handle on its head! The pupa was green at first, but it soon changed to a dark shiny brown.

Sphinx stayed that way all winter long. He hardly moved in his tiny underground cell. He was like a mummy. It snowed and stormed above him, but he was safe and snug eight inches below the snow.

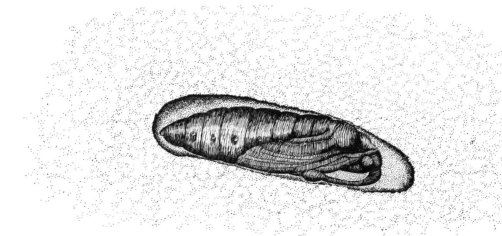

Finally spring came. The snow disappeared as the
sun warmed the earth. Plants began to grow again. The
gardener planted his garden, just as he had done the
year before. He set out tomato plants.

One day in June the pupa began to move. It pushed
and worked its way aboveground. Then the pupal case
split down the back, and Sphinx moth crawled out!

His body was all soft and wet. He had small crumpled
wings on his back. The six true legs of the caterpillar
had changed to six long furry legs. The prolegs had
disappeared entirely.

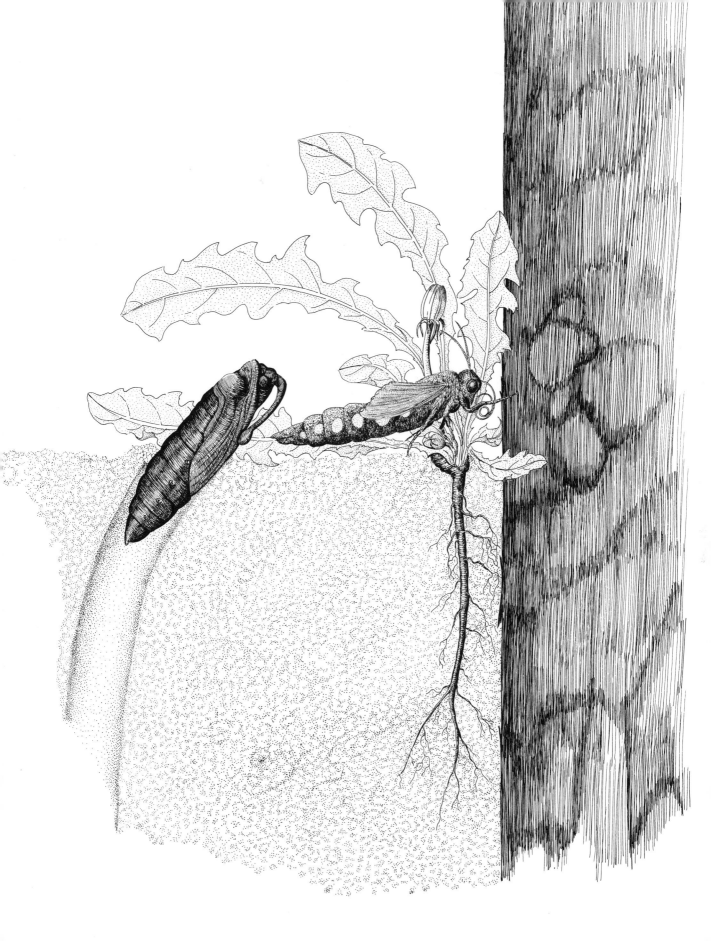

Sphinx moth crawled up a fence post and exercised his tiny wings. Soon they began to get bigger—and bigger—till at last they were full-sized. Then they hardened.

Sphinx was a big gray moth with yellow spots on his body. When he was at rest, he folded his wings over his back. Their pattern and colors were almost exactly the same as those of the old fence post.

When evening came, Sphinx spread his long,
narrow wings and took off. He flew fast and strong,
like a hummingbird.

He flew to the flower garden first. At last he could eat again! But he wouldn't eat tomato leaves now. He uncoiled his tongue to suck nectar.

The tongue was almost four inches long. It had formed in the jug handle on the pupa's head. When he wasn't using it, Sphinx moth coiled up his tongue like a watch spring.

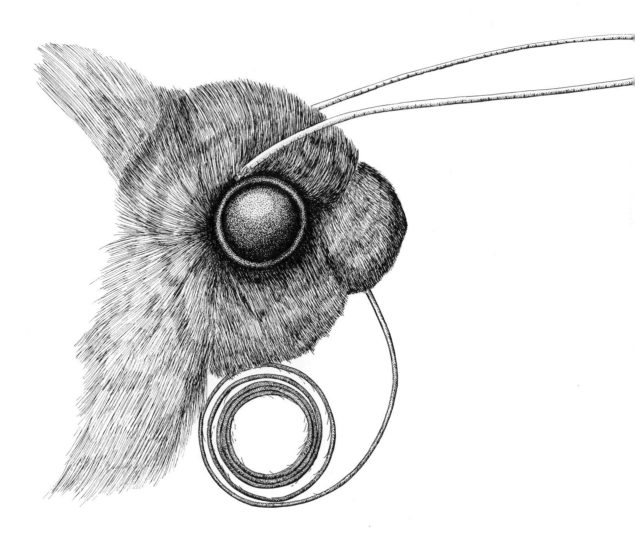

When he had finished feeding, Sphinx flew away
through the dusk in search of a mate. He found one too.
    She came back and laid some eggs on the gardener's
tomato plants the next night. There would be Sphinx
caterpillars on the tomato plants this summer too.